INTO THE GOODHUE COUNTY JAIL:

POEMS TO FREE PRISONERS

JAMES P. LENFESTEY

INTO THE GOODHUE COUNTY JAIL:

POEMS TO FREE PRISONERS

RED DRAGONFLY PRESS — 2008 — MINNESOTA

ISBN: 978-1-890193-73-7

Printed in the United States of America
by BookMobile, a wind-powered company

Text typeset in Melior 8 pt / 13pt
a digital adaptation of metal type designed by Hermann Zapf

Cover and title page lettering is Lancelot Title
a digital adaptation of Duensing Titling designed by Jim Rimmer

Cover photo: Detail of a wall from the Forbidden City in Beijing, China
(stockphoto)

Published by Red Dragonfly Press
press-in-residence at the Anderson Center
P. O. Box 406
Red Wing, MN 55066

For a complete catalogue visit www.reddragonflypress.org

Like a doctor prescribing a medication for each disease,
I use what remedy is at hand to save the world.

— Han-shan

From my monk-like cell at a writing residency at the Anderson Center for Interdisciplinary Arts in Red Wing, Minnesota, as I contemplated the works of ancient Chinese hermit monks and poets, I visited the Goodhue County Jail to talk about writing poetry. These poems are the result of that encounter, real and imagined. They are dedicated to all prisoners of cells exterior and interior, real and imagined.

Gratitude to the Anderson Center for providing me both opportunities.

James P. Lenfestey
Minneapolis, Minnesota
Spring, 2008

CONTENTS

"Don't merely follow in the footsteps of old masters —
Seek what they sought," Bashō wrote 300 years ago
in Japan, and Sam Hamill recited last week in Minnesota.
So I enter the cave called the Goodhue County Jail,
eager to see your cells and compare them to my own.
Ahh, you are lucky! No clutter. Easier, then,
to ask the unasked question. The unanswerable one.
Then wait, by the still pond, for the frog's *kerplunk!*

*Japan's most famous poet wanderer. His most famous haiku:

The old pond
A frog jumped in
Kerplunk.

— Translated by Allen Ginsberg

3

The poet stands before the prisoners,
you with time on your hands, in a shitload of trouble,
me with time on my hands, and no fear.
What could possibly hurt a poet?
That no one pays attention? Ha! We can wait a thousand years.
I'm excited to have an audience, especially a captive one.
For, like you, I relish my day in court. To argue the pain
of absent fathers, the joy of finding the father within.

When you walk out of this jail,
you have four problems.
Where are you going to live?
How will you eat?
Who will be your friend?
To whom can you give your burning love?
I can help with the last one.
Start here, and now, with yourself.
An angel sang this morning. Were you listening?

I heard an angel singing
When the day was springing:
"Mercy, Pity, and Peace,
Are the world's release."

— William Blake

Which of us does not have skin all over his body?
How many of us don't know our father's true face?
Which of us feels no pain pounding beneath our hearts,
screaming through our ribs, wild to get out?
How many of us have no idea why we did
what we did to get here?

You know what a monk is?
Someone who lives in a cell and gets down on his knees.
You know what a prisoner is?
No, not someone locked in jail!
Someone who doesn't embrace the time in his cell
like the lover he has always longed for.

We're all in cells. The skin cell. The blood cell.
The sex cell. The breath cell. The death cell.
Close your eyes. Only then you can hear distant
traffic as a waterfall, the fly's jazzy buzz.
Everything is like something else, even a prison cell.
Pry open your fists, clenched with anger and despair.
Make a basket of your hands, thumbprint brushing thumbprint.
Time is a cell. Meditate inside it until you're free.

Up before dawn, the monk, like you, blinks back the dark.
The monk, like you, stretches sleep-heavy limbs toward the floor.
The monk places his palms together, face up,
breathes in, breathes out, breathes in, breathes out,
swaying to the stroke of the cricket's violin, or still as stone.
Then does push-ups, brushes his teeth, makes his bed.

In orange jumpsuits the color of a monk's one robe,
the quiet ones, like monks, slide from cell to table,
carrying inside them the story which is their life.
They eat slowly, hands careful, then still.
All over America, prisons sprout like monasteries.
First thing in the morning, bells and chanting together.
Then breakfast-thin soup, a steamed white roll bland as stone.
Everyone wipes his own bowl, the day spread out before him.

I hold it up to the light. No one, even in jail,
does not recognize it, this apple. Closing my eyes,
I bounce it off my chest to my other hand,
thumping my sternum with a heart sound.
I do it again, then again, until a rhythm arrives —
a red apple beating from hand to heart to hand.
If you are diligent, you will wake in the morning
with a warm bruise beating beneath your prison togs.

Anyone here who was never born?
Anyone here who's not going to die?
Anyone here who's not puzzled over
what the between part is about?
Then join me, friends, join me in making a book
bound between birth and death.
One with a belly and balls, covered with rough hide
scuffed and scarred over the dark stories inside
where pain and secrets are abundant, the ending still unknown.

It's cheap to do. One pencil, one paper,
one brush, one color,
one needle, one thread,
one hammer, one chisel,   .
four walls of stone.
One hour each morning at dawn,
before the louts begin to yell,
the engines of hell rev.

Few poets dwell where the Prophets do —
in the cloudy heaven of Answers.
Ask a poet, and he will wonder out loud
with you all the way to The End.
It is the questions that keep him on fire
from one millennium to the next. That question
which you have never dared to ask? Ask it now.

Novels are like big-rig trucks — coast-to-coast
contract haulers. Screenplays are corporations, multi-
nationals built from the ground up on one clever invention.
Short stories are entrepreneurs, store fronts with store backs.
Poems are simply a room where your life
depends on each small sound.

Had nothing as a boy. You had more.
He looked into the rich man's keep
and the rich man jailed him.
He worked hard, and saved. Had only one child.
And left behind in every town a library
so you could have the open door he never had.
Before he died, he bought the rich man's keep
and gave it to you. It's open right down the road.

How are the beds? I doubt they are too soft.
And the night? Is it full of screams? Or stone quiet?
And the stars, do they not still shine over your head?
And the dawn, does it not come as slowly every day?
Does a bird ever enter the jail yard? If so, does it ever sing?
Could it sing, night after night from your hard bed?

Research has revealed that abused children never understand metaphor.
Do you not see that the stars, and the space between, are your life?
That the river flowing nearby, murky with snags,
moves toward the ocean's salty Heaven?
Tell me what happened to you that you cannot see
that the leaf turning brown and brittle is your mother's hand?
That the taillights vanishing red in the night are your father's eyes?
Did the fist of his absence hit you that hard?

I'm a poet. Do you know what a poet is?
A joke so lame late show comedians won't even attempt it.
A profession fathers don't even bother to warn their children against.
The hard work we do digs deep into darkness, ending God knows where.
Mr. Blake spent his nights absorbed in visions no on else could see.
Poets don't care one whit if you sit in stubborn silence all day.
We can wait.
For you to touch the end of a golden thread.
Follow the tangled ball it leads you into.
Discover the Heaven that lies beyond.

> *I give you the end of a golden string;*
> *Only wind it into a ball,*
> *It will lead you in at Heaven's gate*
> *Built in Jerusalem's wall.*

—William Blake, "Jerusalem"

Fathers who stayed. They hug their wives and kids,
then leave for work, plowing distant fields, fighting the Emperor's wars.
But then return. Maybe late for supper, frayed as old wire,
but there they stand, feeding the hungry hole behind your eyes.
Yesterday I watched two husbands send their wives off for a month of art.
It's alright, dear, I can handle the kids, the diabetic cat,
the loony mother-in-law and the silent dad. If you
can handle the stillness, the garden of delicious sound.

CLOSE YOUR EYES

Close your eyes and draw a picture
of your father. Some have big bellies,
some no faces, some big fists.
Some are round, eating your food.
Some pencil thin, starving for you.
Some radiate daggers like darts,
or sunbeams like daggers.
Some disappear into a tiny dot.

21

Begin here: "If I found my father, I . . ."
Begin here: "In return for my father's love, I . . ."
Begin here: "If I had a son, I . . ."
When I look at my father, it is like looking
into a blazing sun or a deep well, only the edges seen.
Close your eyes and look at your father.
Close your eyes and hold your son.

Dragon's breath roars up your bulging forearm scars.
In the outside world, where the walls are inside,
such a beast never backs down, never cools off.
Inside these walls of stone, your hands offer the first poem,
its heart writhing on the page like dragon fire.
Tonight as I gaze out the dark window,
something bright streaks across the sky — a man
riding a dragon's broad back, breathing free.

So often we forget what we are good at.
I remember the rim of the canyon, lighting
the fire, beans bubbling in the ragged can,
wondering with him at the sweep of stars.
He remembers, he wrote me in a poem,
that I knew what the stone kiva was for,
why the Colorado River turned green.

Loved me, from before I was born to the day he died —
this son who would carry his happy name through time.
His first son dead, and so this second, the shy, sickly one,
with shoulders built of thin, protruding bones.
I feel him now looking over my shoulder,
tears streaming down his cheeks. Of happiness
I always thought, not knowing he remembered another son
with small sturdy shoulders buried in the garden.

Was someone else's son.
When you brought the cracked bat down,
who was over your shoulder, guiding your arm?
Which way was he pulling: back, or down?
Alcohol was involved, of course. And meth
these days. But the arms over the shoulder
are always there, pulling one way or the other.

Skinny son of a happy, prosperous father.
How you hated me on sight.
We never even spoke. Except, perhaps, for
an "Excuse me" passing in a smoky bar.
You wanted to kill me right then, the way
I walked, heel to toe, shouting I had a father.

That money you stole was your father's money,
his thin wallet a bitter, dry plain,
a plague of locusts eating everything within.
You trudged every morning to school
with sad, empty pockets, heavy with longing
for the lightness of gold.

Oh my god, the red one. Hot-wired and
fast around curves.
And yes, you deserved it, that prick
who parked it there
knowing all along that it belonged to you,
it's radiant grille designed like a smile
to flash all over the fast countryside.

Served time in silence, alone in a room, penitent.
So still, the traffic of the world breaks into voices —
a cardinal's whistle, a skittering leaf, a chrysalis splitting its skin.
We grieve for crimes in a world now not our own.
The ground-hugging thrush snatched by the feral cat.
The coyote blinded by poison, leg gnawed by traps.
The Monarch butterfly felled by ants sawing his wings to bits.
The soldier retrieved under fire, abandoned at home.

My uniform reduced to jeans and several tees,
my number — 2 — stenciled on the door.
Both my window and my door open
to the changing world, where a car will take me home.
But I feel I am at home, here, contemplating the news
my fingers uncover while thinking of you,
my cellmates, in your stone house down the hill.

Outside the window of my cell, a ragged branch
rattles its leaves, yellow and curling from the tips.
Maple leaves redden against a dull sky behind.
Sentenced to 31 days in a room with only pen and books,
I become your friend. Every day I see your leaves
let go and scuttle like mice over the metal roof below.
Growing emptiness is our life's work.

Steady work, this poetry.
Every night, late, or every morning, early,
with the busy world settled to a forgotten dot or hum.
No sense saving it up, there's always more.
The dark well has no bottom, the dark sky boundless space.
No wages, but no cost. A bit of ink, a scrap of paper,
courage to climb down, wings to slowly rise.

I am an orchard in full bloom, fruit dropping from my fingertips
faster than bushels can catch. Every sound a melody.
Every bit of dust a fleck of marble or mercury or gold.
Every dry or colored leaf a page torn from an ancient book.
Fire burns in the furnace of my skin. Lights off I glow.
Who knows if others will warm at these flames, taste this fruit.
But I am nourished now, so hot and ripe
the sky darkens every night to contain me in my cell.

When the stone gate finally opens, will you be ready?
Ready to carry your cell's stillness in your flaming palms?
Your girlfriend, will she feel your calm?
The rusty car, will it run more smoothly?
Will your father, lost at sea, turn toward you from his watery bed?
Will your mother, exhausted from the second shift, sleep content?
Will you find in every sound around you a treasure for the chest
buried deep inside you? Will you be listening? *Kerplunk!*

The complete teachings of all Buddhas
— past, present and future —
are to be found within the essence
of every human being."

— Hui Neng

THE POETRY OF ZEN, translated and edited by Sam Hamill and J.P. Seaton, Shambhala Publications, 2004

THE RAG AND BONE SHOP OF THE HEART: POEMS FOR MEN, edited by Robert Bly, James Hillman, Michael Meade, HarperCollins, 1992

COLD MOUNTAIN: 100 POEMS BY THE T'ANG DYNASTY POET HAN-SHAN, translated by Burton Watson, Columbia University Press, 1970

Libraries should have these, and many more books of poetry, or often will order specific volumes if you ask. Purchase your own copies when you can and carry them with you. Or copy your favorite poems into a notebook. Read them over from time to time. Memorize your favorites and recite them to strangers. Some poems will become teachers. Some strangers will become friends.